Parsing lessons for young children: resolved into their elements, for the assistance of parents and teachers. By Mrs. Lovechild.

Mrs. Lovechild

ECCO
PRINT EDITIONS

Parsing lessons for young children: resolved into their elements, for the assistance of parents and teachers. By Mrs. Lovechild.
Lovechild, Mrs.
ESTCID: T113069
Reproduction from British Library
Mrs. Lovechild = Eleanor Fenn. With a final leaf of advertisements.
London : printed for E. Newbery, 1798.
xiv,56,[2]p. ; 18°

ECCO

Eighteenth Century Collections Online Print Editions

Gale ECCO Print Editions

Relive history with *Eighteenth Century Collections Online*, now available in print for the independent historian and collector. This series includes the most significant English-language and foreign-language works printed in Great Britain during the eighteenth century, and is organized in seven different subject areas including literature and language; medicine, science, and technology; and religion and philosophy. The collection also includes thousands of important works from the Americas.

The eighteenth century has been called "The Age of Enlightenment." It was a period of rapid advance in print culture and publishing, in world exploration, and in the rapid growth of science and technology – all of which had a profound impact on the political and cultural landscape. At the end of the century the American Revolution, French Revolution and Industrial Revolution, perhaps three of the most significant events in modern history, set in motion developments that eventually dominated world political, economic, and social life.

In a groundbreaking effort, Gale initiated a revolution of its own: digitization of epic proportions to preserve these invaluable works in the largest online archive of its kind. Contributions from major world libraries constitute over 175,000 original printed works. Scanned images of the actual pages, rather than transcriptions, recreate the works ***as they first appeared.***

Now for the first time, these high-quality digital scans of original works are available via print-on-demand, making them readily accessible to libraries, students, independent scholars, and readers of all ages.

For our initial release we have created seven robust collections to form one the world's most comprehensive catalogs of 18th century works.

Initial Gale ECCO Print Editions collections include:

History and Geography

Rich in titles on English life and social history, this collection spans the world as it was known to eighteenth-century historians and explorers. Titles include a wealth of travel accounts and diaries, histories of nations from throughout the world, and maps and charts of a world that was still being discovered. Students of the War of American Independence will find fascinating accounts from the British side of conflict.

Social Science

Delve into what it was like to live during the eighteenth century by reading the first-hand accounts of everyday people, including city dwellers and farmers, businessmen and bankers, artisans and merchants, artists and their patrons, politicians and their constituents. Original texts make the American, French, and Industrial revolutions vividly contemporary.

Medicine, Science and Technology

Medical theory and practice of the 1700s developed rapidly, as is evidenced by the extensive collection, which includes descriptions of diseases, their conditions, and treatments. Books on science and technology, agriculture, military technology, natural philosophy, even cookbooks, are all contained here.

Literature and Language

Western literary study flows out of eighteenth-century works by Alexander Pope, Daniel Defoe, Henry Fielding, Frances Burney, Denis Diderot, Johann Gottfried Herder, Johann Wolfgang von Goethe, and others. Experience the birth of the modern novel, or compare the development of language using dictionaries and grammar discourses.

Religion and Philosophy

The Age of Enlightenment profoundly enriched religious and philosophical understanding and continues to influence present-day thinking. Works collected here include masterpieces by David Hume, Immanuel Kant, and Jean-Jacques Rousseau, as well as religious sermons and moral debates on the issues of the day, such as the slave trade. The Age of Reason saw conflict between Protestantism and Catholicism transformed into one between faith and logic -- a debate that continues in the twenty-first century.

Law and Reference

This collection reveals the history of English common law and Empire law in a vastly changing world of British expansion. Dominating the legal field is the *Commentaries of the Law of England* by Sir William Blackstone, which first appeared in 1765. Reference works such as almanacs and catalogues continue to educate us by revealing the day-to-day workings of society.

Fine Arts

The eighteenth-century fascination with Greek and Roman antiquity followed the systematic excavation of the ruins at Pompeii and Herculaneum in southern Italy; and after 1750 a neoclassical style dominated all artistic fields. The titles here trace developments in mostly English-language works on painting, sculpture, architecture, music, theater, and other disciplines. Instructional works on musical instruments, catalogs of art objects, comic operas, and more are also included.

2

PARSING LESSONS

FOR

YOUNG CHILDREN:

RESOLVED INTO

THEIR ELEMENTS,

FOR THE

ASSISTANCE

OF

PARENTS AND TEACHERS;

BY

MRS. LOVECHILD.

LONDON:

PRINTED FOR E. NEWBERY, THE CORNER
OF ST. PAUL'S CHURCH-YARD.

1798.

TO

MOTHERS, GOVERNESSES,

ASSISTANTS,

AND

ALL WHO ARE ENGAGED IN THE

TASK OF TEACHING,

THIS LITTLE WORK,

TO EASE THEIR LABOUR, AND SPARE THEIR

TIME,

IS INSCRIBED,

WITH A SINCERE WISH FOR SUCCESS

IN THE ATTEMPT

TO RENDER THE STUDY OF GRAMMAR

PLEASANT.

PREFACE.

THOSE Ladies who have not in their early years ſtudied Grammar with much aſſiduity, are unwilling to enter upon the taſk of teaching it I will ſay more—they are unable; for, however a perſon may, from being converſant with the beſt authors, fall habitually into a tolerable degree of correctneſs in ſpeaking and writing; yet, without a clear idea of the Principles of Grammar, ſhe cannot inſtruct her Children at an early age. Few, therefore, make the attempt; and yet fewer ſucceed Ladies view it as an arduous undertaking, and are fearful of engaging in it; and thoſe who enter upon it proceed with timidity, loſing all that heart-felt ſatisfaction which ſhould attend a Mother who is conſcious ſhe is fulfilling her duty to a darling Child

The writer of this little volume is happy in an aſſurance, that her endeavours to aſſiſt young Ladies in their attempts to teach their children, have been acceptable. The office ſhe has aſſumed is an humble one—that of

Dame behind the curtain, to prompt such Mothers as are diffident of themselves Certainly Providence designed our early youth should be under the guidance of Females; they must supply milk; they must support the tottering steps of infancy, in a figurative, as well as a literal sense. Men of learning are incapable of stooping sufficiently low to conduct those who are but entering the paths,—a sprightly young Woman, who will condescend to avail herself of the experience of an old one, is the person to initiate young students—I am the old Woman who offer my service, and flatter myself with the hope of leading the dear little people with ease and satisfaction

A great love for Children, and affection for such Mothers as I see attentive to their offspring, makes me earnestly wish to serve both. This cannot be done more effectually than by awakening in the breast of youthful Parents an early and high idea of their sacred and important trust—by persuading them to esteem nothing a trifle, which concerns their Children.

It

It is not so much the pushing Children forward, that is the desirable object, as rendering the entrance pleasant, and so making them delight in the paths of learning, by gentle degrees inducing habits of application, which, in maturer years, may lead our Pupils to high degrees of honour.

If I have any conceit, it is that I have acquired a knack of communicating the little knowledge which I possess, so as to be intelligible to the capacities, and agreeable to the taste of infantine Pupils, if I have any thing to boast, it is, that I dare hazard the sneer of those who, in a lounging humour, may take up my little volume—But let us defy scorn, and attend to the lovely objects of this publication

Children, if you expect them to read with spirit and propriety, must be supplied with lessons suited to their taste, that is, *prattle*, like their own Parsing Lessons, too, must be adapted to the tender age of the Pupil. If a sentence be not perfectly level to the capacity of our young Grammarian, how is it possible that he should resolve it into the elements

elements of which it is composed? No; Parsing Lessons for a Child must be in the most easy and simple language—such are now offered

By the help of these, a Lady may examine the progress of her children, without trouble, and even without previous knowledge of Grammar.

This is designed to be a sequel, or rather companion, to The Child's Grammar, in which the little people study and The Mother's Grammar, which consists of extracts from our best writers on the subject, arranged in such a manner as to facilitate the task of teaching, to such Mothers as have themselves neglected attending to Grammar, by sparing them the labour of seeking in various books for their own information, and I flatter myself it has saved much trouble to those who are the best informed on the subject my leisure is well employed, if it can spare the more valuable time of Mothers of Families

The expedience of initiating a Boy before his entrance upon School, cannot be disputed a previous knowledge of rudiments, spares

ſpares him many unpleaſant hours, which the brighteſt and moſt diligent Child muſt experience, before he can acquire any clear idea—if indeed they who begin their ſchool exerciſe with minds totally uninformed, ever do acquire ſuch.

Reſpecting Boys, a freſh difficulty ariſes to a Mother ſhe is apprehenſive that the little volume which enables her to inſtruct her Daughter, may not accord with the Grammar which will be put into the hands of her little Son, at his entrance into School: but this difficulty is now happily removed, by the very recent appearance of a ſmall Publication, namely, "Rudiments of Engliſh "*Grammar, for the Uſe of Schools*" its Author is the Rev. H S I Bullen—This proves that a learned Man can ſtoop—but there is ſtill need of a Dame, to conduct young Students, till a Superior ſhall deign to take them by the hand. allow me to lead them to ſuch Tutors, and my office is fulfilled.

ADVER-

ADVERTISEMENT.

THE Child's Grammar, and Mother's Grammar, being ſuch ſmall publications, it has been thought better to refer to them than to ſwell this little work with ſuch particulars as are to be fonnd in thoſe diminutive volumes, of which the price is ſo inconſiderable, that no Mother, who approves the mode of inſtruction adopted by the Writer, will neglect to procure them

Yet the explanation of the Parts of Speech is inſerted in the beginning, and ſome few other paſſages, ſo as to render this little volume quite ſufficient by itſelf, for the purpoſe for which it is deſigned

The Parſing Leſſons are in Sets; and there is prefixed to each a ſhort explanation of the method in which that Set is deſigned to be uſed

For early Leſſons, to give variety, and to multiply the very eaſy ones, a Lady who may chooſe to attend ſo far, can produce The Infant's Friend, Part I —She will ſay—

" Find

"Find the nouns in this ſet of words as you read them —Now find the verbs," &c —— Part II affords very eaſy Parſing Leſſons in the Short Sentences, the Reading Leſſons in Part II. may be uſed too, by thoſe who are more advanced, as Parſing Leſſons.

To return to the preſent work.

In theſe examples, various modes are uſed to vary the taſk in ſome Leſſons, the Parts of Speech are marked by figures; in theſe a Child may, by means of a ſlip, amuſe himſelf by trying his own ſkill.

The ſame method may be purſued in thoſe where the Words are placed in columns, and the Part of Speech put oppoſite—a young Pupil only to tell the Part of Speech; and even thoſe who are more advanced, ſhould go through them the firſt time only naming the Part of Speech, and aſſigning the reaſon why it is ſuch; the ſecond time, he may explain further particulars thus two children may be examined at the ſame time, though their progreſs be not the ſame; for example, take a noun and verb; for inſtance,

"Lambs bleat"

A young Child.

Lambs—noun, we ſee them, &c.

An elder one.

Lambs—plural nominative—going before the verb anſwering the queſtion *what*.

A young Child

bleat—verb—it is ſomething which they *do*.

An elder.

Plural agreeing with the nominative Lambs *Third perſon*—*Indicative* mode, as it declares ſomething—*Preſent* tenſe; it means now, at this time.

"We ſit here"

We—a pronoun, uſed inſtead of our names—*Plural* number, as it ſpeaks of more than one—*Nominative* caſe, it goes before the verb, and anſwers to the queſtion *Who.*—Who ſit here? We do—firſt perſon.

ſit—a verb, it is ſomething which we do—*Plural* number, agreeing with its nominative—*Indicative* mode; it declares—*Preſent* tenſe, now.

here;

here; to a *young* Child a particle, to an *elder* an adverb, meaning *in this place*, so expressing in one word what would require several —*See Child's Grammar*, p 18

In the respective Lessons, a reference is given to the little Grammars, to enable the Pupils to consult the passages, and prepare themselves.

It is always a good method to assign a reason why a word is such or such a part of speech, and the same respecting all its circumstances, where the Pupil is sufficiently advanced.

Example.

"Come hither to me"

To a young Child.

Come—a verb, it is something which you do; it can be added to a pronoun—I come, thou comest, &c—*To an elder*, it is imperative mode, it commands—second person—come thou, or do thou come.

to—a preposition, shewing the relation, &c

To a young Child

me—a pronoun; it is uſed inſtead of my name—*To an elder*, it is accuſative, following the prepoſition *to*—it is firſt perſon—ſingular number.

"My mamma teaches me."

My—a pronoun.

mamma—a noun, becauſe a perſon—Who teaches you?—Mamma—Mamma, then, is the nominative caſe, becauſe it anſwers the queſtion *Who*

teaches—a verb, governed by the nominative, mamma—Mamma teaches me

me—a pronoun—accuſative, as it follows the verb—ſingular, as it ſpeaks of one only

What perſon is to be uſed for mamma?

All nouns are of the third perſon

What pronoun would you uſe before the verb? She

What pronoun after the verb?

Her.

She is very kind, and I love *her*.

PARSING LESSONS

FOR

YOUNG CHILDREN.

PARTS OF SPEECH.

THERE are ten parts of ſpeech—article, noun, adjective, pronoun, verb, participle, adverb, conjunction, prepoſition, interjection.

1 ARTICLE.

They are a, an, the—theſe are ſet before nouns to fix their meaning.

2. NOUN.

A noun is the name of a perſon, place, or thing—Whatever you can ſee, hear, feel, or underſtand, is a noun.

3. ADJECTIVE.

An adjective is a word that denotes the quality of any perſon, place, or thing.

4. PRONOUN.

A pronoun is a word uſed inſtead of a noun.

5. VERB.

A verb is a word that denotes the acting or being of any perſon, place, or thing.

Thus far the Pupil to learn perfectly by rote. The reſt ſhould be called Particles—words which he cannot yet learn, if the Child be young, and this be the firſt time of his going through the book. For ſuch Grammarians one would wiſh to avoid participles; yet they will call them verbs with ing or ed; or adjectives when joined to a noun.

PAR-

PARTICLES.

6. PARTICIPLE.

A participle is ſometimes an adjective derived of a verb, at others, a verb with the idea of time annexed—and at others, a kind of noun.

7. ADVERB.

An adverb is a part of ſpeech joined to a verb, an adjective, a participle, and ſometimes to another adverb, to expreſs the manner or circumſtance of it.

8 CONJUNCTION.

Conjunctions join words or ſentences together.

9 PREPOSITION.

Prepoſitions are ſet before nouns and pronouns, to expreſs the relation of perſons, places or things to each other.

10. INTERJECTION

An interjection is a word thrown in to express any sudden emotion of the mind; but not necessary to the sense.

In fact, an interjection is no part of speech—they being, in many instances, mere sounds; and the same in all languages

The articles are easily remembered, and can afterwards be explained —*Mother's Grammar, page* 12.

Of a noun a Child can very early conceive an idea, if the Teacher will confine herself to such as are objects of sense

Of a verb you may give Children an idea by keeping them long to active verbs, or at least common ones, and by telling them that *I*, *he*, &c. &c. can be prefixed to no other kind of words.

Pronouns may be explained familiarly after a time but it muſt be remarked by every one who is converſant with Infants, that they make no uſe of pronouns till they are taught to do it.

Adjectives may be taught by examples and frequent explanation.

The reſt muſt be ſunk to a very young Scholar, as words which at preſent he cannot underſtand—and compriſed under the general name of Particles.

PRELUDE TO FIRST LESSON.

Child's Gram. page 1. | *Mother's Gram. page 13.*

The room is full of nouns; you cannot turn your head but you ſee one—the *table*, the *chair*, &c—theſe you *ſee*, they are therefore nouns.

Nouns.

Perſons. Brother ſiſter couſin nurſe child ſervant farmer.

Places. Garden parlour chamber city pariſh village.

Things. Baſket kettle carpet letter ſofa cuſhion.

—*The four firſt pages of Infant's Friend, Part II.*

I can ſhew you theſe, or pictures of them—we can have no pictures of any words but nouns.

Child's

Child's Gram 2. *Mother's Gram 14.*

Nouns common

Man woman town book table ſervant porter girl.

Nouns proper

Ann Elizabeth Iſabella London England Dover.

I.

Article.	*Noun.*	*Article.*	*Noun.*
An	apple	the	garden
a	barrow	a	field
a	chaiſe	the	parlour
the	coach	a	meadow
an	orange	a	chamber
a	parrot	a	cloſet
a	farmer	a	woman
a	ſervant	a	ſoldier
a	child	a	nurſe.

II.

Child's Gram. 3. *Mother's Gram* 17.

Adjectives.

Good naughty dull ſweet pretty great wiſe high.

Art	*Adj*	*Noun.*	*Art.*	*Adj.*	*Noun.*
A	ripe	plum	a	good	boy
a	neat	girl	a	blue	coat
an	old	gown	a	warm	cloak
the	old	horſe	the	black	dog
a	white	frock	a	black	ſcarf
a	ſoft	peach	a	hard	pear.

See ſhort ſentences, Infant's Friend, Part II.

Think of ſome epithets for my gown—It is *new—neat—pretty—fine—clear—long.* Think of ſome for the kitten—It is *briſk, ſmall, young, white.*

III.

Verb.

Child's Gram. 6. *Mother's Gram. 22.*

Whatever you do is a verb.

Verbs.

Play run jump ſing dance read walk ride come talk have grow beat lend meet ſpeak throw ſtand think draw bring carry creep break.

Birds *ſing*. Boys *talk*. Babes *cry*.

You can place a pronoun before a verb, or after it. So learn the pronouns.

Singular.		*Singular.*	
1.	I	1.	Me
2.	thou	2.	thee
3.	he, ſhe, it	3.	him, her, it
Plural.		*Plural*	
1.	We	1.	Us
2.	ye	2.	you
3.	they.	3.	them.

IV. *

Noun	*Verb*	*Pronoun.*	*Verb.*
Lambs	bleat	I	write
cats	mew	you	read
dogs	bark	I	teach
hens	cluck	you	learn
babes	cry	we	ſit
men	ſpeak.	they	walk

V.

Article	*Noun*	*Verb.*	*Noun.*
The	cat	kills	mice
a	hen	lays	eggs
the	cows	give	milk
a	ſheep	has	wool
the	horſe	eats	graſs
the	bees	collect	honey.

* *The ſecond time, the mode may be explained; the third time, the tenſe, indicative preſent.*

VI.

VI.

Article	*Noun*	*Verb*	*Adjective.*
The	graſs	is	green
an	aſs	is	patient
the	horſes	are	ready
a	dog	is	faithful
a	wolf	is	fierce
a	cow	is	uſeful

VII *

Noun	*Verb*	*Participle.*	*Noun*
Owls	fly	by	night
rooks	eat	- - -	grubs
fiſh	ſwim	in	water
hogs	roll	in	mire
children	go	to	ſchool
calves	ſuck	- - -	milk

* *Child's Gram.* 19. *Mother's Gram.* 55.
Prepoſition.

VIII.

Child's Gram 15. *Mother's Gram* 53

Verb	*Adverb.*	*Verb.*	*Adverb.*
Come	quickly	come	ſoon
go	directly	ring	twice
riſe	early	behave	well
write	correctly	ſpeak	civilly
read	ſlowly	look	modeſtly
ſpeak	gently.	eat	moderately.

IX

Noun	*Verb*	*Prep*	*Ar*	*Noun*
Birds	build	in	---	trees
hens	lay	on	the	ground
hawks	ſoar	in	the	air.
ſpiders	ſpin	in	---	corners
foxes	burrow	in	the	earth
moles	live	under	---	ground

X.

Noun	*Verb.*	*Part*	*Prep.*	*Art.*	*Noun*
Silk	is	ſpun	by	a	worm
hemp	is	peeled	from	a	plant
flax	is	peeled	from	a	plant
cotton	is	produced	from	---	plants
muſlin	is	made	of	---	cotton
wool	is	ſhorne	from	---	ſheep
leather	is	made	of	---	ſkins
ſnow	is	kept	in	the	ice-houſe
ſalmon	are	brought	from	---	town
carp	are	caught	in	the	canal
deer	are	fed	in	the	park
veniſon	is	ſent	to	---	friends
mutton	is	ſold	in	the	market
horſes	are	bought	in	the	fair.

XI.

Adjective	*Noun*	*Preposition*	*Pronoun*	*Noun*
good	example	of	your	parents
kind	advice	of	your	friends
grateful	- - - -	to	your	parents
obedient	- - - -	to	them	
diligent	- - - -	at	your	book
active	- - - -	in	your	business.

XII.

obliging	caution	from	your	companions
affectionate	- - - -	to	your	sisters
mild	- - - -	in	your	behaviour
gentle	- - - -	to	your	playfellows
thankful	- - - -	to	your	friends
civil	hint	from	your	schoolfellows.

THIS book being designed for Children of different ages, examples are given of every part of speech, but it cannot be too often inculcated, that beginners must long be kept to the five first; of which they may be led to conceive a clear idea, and in them should enter upon no distinction the first time of going through them.

In the following set of lessons the younger Pupils must leave all beyond 5 as particles.

All should acquire the names by rote very perfectly, article, noun, &c. *only very young ones must not attempt to distinguish beyond the* verb.

To be acquired perfectly by rote.

Article, noun, adjective, pronoun, verb, participle, adverb, conjunction, preposition, interjection.

The Teacher should condescend to imprint this succession firmly in her memory.

1. Article.
2. Noun.
3. Adjective.
4. Pronoun
5. Verb
6. Participle
7. Adverb
8. Conjunction.
9. Preposition.
10. Interjection.

The

The Manner of using the following Set

Read the sentence aloud first; then take a slip of stiff paper, or card, with a perforation just large enough to exhibit a figure, place it so as to conceal the upper row.

" *What part of speech is* be?"—*The Child answers* " a verb "—*You move the slip, and shew him the figure* 5.—a, *an article*—*You move it, and shew him the figure* 1—*and so proceed to the end of that sentence,—then read another; and so on.*

LESSONS.

I.

5 1 3 2
Be a good child.

5 8 4 5 4
Do as I bid you.

5 4 5 2
Let us lay words.

5 9 5 7
Strive to learn quickly.

5 2 5 2
Let Elizabeth ſpell nouns.

5 2 5 2
Let Ann arrange words.

5 2 5 2
Let John parſe leſſons.

5 9 4 3 2
Look at your little grammar.

5 1 2 9 4 3 2
Learn a piece of it every day

II

II.

1 2 5 9 4 8 5
The horſe works for us, ſo does

1 3 2 2 5 4 3
the poor aſs. Cows give us nice

2 2 5 4 2 2
milk. Sheep yield us wool. Deer

5 4 2 8 2 1 2
give us food and clothes; the fleſh

5 2 1 2 5 2 8
is veniſon, the ſkin is leather; and

4 5 2 9 1 2 8
we make jelly of the horns; and

3 3 2 2 9
many uſeful things. Bones of

2 5 6 9 3
animals are made into various

2 2 5 1 2 9
things. Ivory is the tooth of

1 2
an elephant.

III.

4 5 9 4 2 5 7
I ſtand behind your chair· do not

5 9 4 5 7 5 9
lean againſt it; do not climb upon

1 2
the ſeat.

7 5 1 2 5 4 9
Where is the baby? Is ſhe with

2 5 4 6 3 7
nurſe? Have you been good whilſt

4 5 9 2
I was at church?

4 5 7 4 2 5
Who knows where my baſket is?

5 4 5 9 5 9 1
Do you wiſh to play in the

2 5 5 4 2
garden? Go, get your hat.

IV.

IV.

1 2 5 1 3 2 8
The fox is a cunning thief; and

2 7 4 5 7 5 2
men, when they do not fear God,

5 3 8 3 1 2
are crafty and deceitful The wolf

5 3 8 3 8 4
is cruel and blood-thirſty. As he

5 1 2 8 5 3 2
devoureth the lamb, ſo do bad men

5 8 5 3 8 3
oppreſs and tear innocent and helpleſs

2 8 4 5 3 9 5
people. Yet it is better to be

1 3 9 2 2 7
the pooreſt of Chriſt's flock than

9 5 3 8 3 8 1
to be proud and cruel as the

2 8 2 4 5 7
lion and tyger, who go about

6 4 4 5 5
ſeeking whom they may devour.

The Book of Nature.

V.

1 2 5 1 3 3 3
The bee is a poor little brown

2 8 4 5 1 3 9 3
inſect; yet it is the wiſeſt of all

2 8 5 1 2 9
inſects: ſo is the nightingale with

4 3 2 4 5 1
its muſical notes, which fill the

2 8 5 1 2 9 1
woods and charm the ear in the

2 1 3 3 2 7 8
ſpring, a little brown bird, not ſo

3 8 1 2 1 2
handſome as a ſparrow. The bee

5 1 2 9 2 8 2
is a pattern of diligence and wiſdom.

3 5 1 2 8 3 5
Happy is the man, and happy are

1 2 4 5 8 3 8 9
the people, who are ſo wiſe as to

5 4 1 2
follow ſuch an example.

The Book of Nature

VI.

1	3	2	5	1	2	8
The	whole	world	is	a	picture,	and

3	1	2	4	5	9	4
all	the	things	we	ſee	with	our

2	5	9	1	2	8	5
eyes	ſpeak	to	the	mind,	and	improve

4	8	8	2	8	2
it.	But	neither	children	nor	men

5	5	2	9	1	2
can	get	wiſdom	without	the	help

9	2	4	5	5	9	4
of	God:	we	muſt	pray	to	Him,

8	4	5	5	8	5
that	we	may	hear	and	underſtand.

Preface to the Book of Nature, or the true Senſe of Things explained and made eaſy to the Capacities of Children: in Two Parts. 1s. 8d.

It is thought that the different methods used in parsing will serve not only to vary the employment to a Child, and so prevent satiety, but likewise operate in creating a quickness.

In the following set, the different parts of speech are marked by being printed in Italics.

The method of using them is this:—The Teacher to read aloud a sentence; then require of the Pupil to say which words are nouns, *or which are* adjectives, *&c* —*The first lessons are of* nouns.

PRELUDE TO THE LESSONS OF NOUNS.

Now, Elizabeth, I think you can pick out the nouns in a ſentence· I will try you by reading ſome

EXAMPLES:

John is gone to *London.*

ELIZ.—*John* is a noun—the *name* of a perſon. *London* too—it is the *name* of a place.

ANN.—*John* is a *proper* name; ſo is *London*

2.

My *brother* has loſt his *book.*

ELIZ.—*Book* is a noun—it is a thing, and *brother* is a perſon—ſo *brother* is a noun.

3.

Take an *apple* Play with your *doll.* I met a *man* in the *field*, and he had a *rake* in his *hand.*

Eliz.—*Apple* and *doll* are nouns—I can *ſee* them, *man*, is a perſon; *field*, a place; *rake* and *hand* are nouns. I can *feel* your hand.

LESSONS OF NOUNS.

I.

The *horſe* eats *graſs* · ſo does the *cow* and the *aſs* and the *deer.* *Goats* brouſe upon *leaves.* *Dogs*, *cats*, and *foxes* eat *fleſh.* *Birds* eat *worms* and *ſeeds* and *fruit.* *Birds* lay *eggs*, and hatch them; they bring *food* to their young *ones* *Beaſts* have *milk*, and let their young *ones* ſuck it. Small *birds* ſing to their *mates* *Fowls* ſeek for *food*, and call their *chicks* to eat it *Ducks* lead their *ducklings* to the *pond.* The *ſwan* makes a large *neſt.*

II.

II

Nouns.

My *doll* is made of *wood.* Mine is of *wax* I have a *doll* made of *rag* Have you a *baby-houſe?* Yes, I have two *rooms.* In the *parlour* there is a *ſofa*, and there are ſix *chairs*, and two *tables*, and a *carpet.* My *ſiſter* drew ſome *pictures*; and my *brother* made *ſtands* for *flowers.*

III.

Adjectives.

Let us make a doll's feaſt We will— I have ſome *pretty* diſhes, and look at this *nice* table how *neat* the cloth is! What ſhall we have? We will have *white* ſoup, a *ſmall* fowl, *young* rabbits, and a *fine* piece of beef, and we will make ſome *new* tarts. Do not make them too *ſweet.* This fruit is too *ripe.* Here are *green* currants, and *red* plums. That apple is *rotten.* Get ſome *freſh* ones Theſe are much *better.* I like orange tarts *beſt*

IV.

Adjectives.

DOLL.

I muſt keep her *cool* and *dry*; elſe this *nice pink* colour will be loſt. What a *neat* coat! I like *blue* ſilk. When ſhe is *good*, ſhe ſhall go abroad, and ſit on this *low* ſeat by me. Hèr cloak is *white*. Look at her muff; it is ſo *pretty*: how *ſoft* and *warm*! Her hat is very *ſmart*. This cap is but a *ſhabby* one. This is her *beſt* gown it is my *dear* mamma's work. Her *worſt* hat is *green*: ſhe has a *new* coat: her *old* one is worn out.

V.

Pronouns.

BIRD.

A boy was walking with *his* mamma; and *he* ſaw a bird fly paſt with a worm in *its* mouth.—Is not that bird hungry, ſaid *he*; for *I* ſee that *he* carries *his* meat paſt in *his* mouth.

It

It is a mother-bird, replied *his* mamma; and *ſhe* is going to feed *her* young; the old birds take unwearied pains to ſupply *their* neſtlings with food. *you* would like to ſee *them* *they* ſit in turn.

Let *us* go, mamma; ſhew *me* the neſt.

No, *my* dear, *we* ſhould frighten *them*—but look! there is the mate · *I* ſaw *him* fly.

VI.

Pronouns continued.

NEST

The old birds make neſts for *their* young, and line *them* with wool and other ſoft things, *they* will even pluck the down from *their* own breaſts *that which you* ſaw has given the worm to *her* neſtlings, and is now flown paſt *us* to ſeek for more *her* mate, mean while, will watch *their* neſt, and chear *her* with a ſong at *her* return; liſten, and *you* will hear *her* greet *him* with a chirp.

VII

Verbs.

THE WOODEN HORSE

A little boy talks to his wooden horſe

Come, Sir, *walk* and *trot*, *let* me *ſee* how you *move*, I *will rub* you down, and *give* you oats and hay, and *will chop* ſtraw for you I *will be* good to you, I *will* not *whip* nor *ſpur* you, nor *let* the hair *rub* off; I *will feed* and *tend* you, and I *will* not *ride* hard and *hurt* your feet, nor *trot* on hard road, ſo as to *make* your feet ſore, nor *hold* the bridle careleſsly and *throw* you down and *cut* your knees. I *will pat* your neck when I *get* up, and *teach* you to *know* me, ſo that you *will turn* your head, and *ſeem* to *like* that I *ſhould mount* I *will ſee* that your hay and corn *are* good, and your bed *is* comfortable, and Tom *muſt waſh* the hot ſand out of your feet, elſe they will *ache*, and you *will grow* lame.

VIII

Verbs continued.

THE INFANT.

Little babies never *ſee* nor *take* notice of any thing that *paſſes*. When your brother *is* as old as you *are*, *aſk* him if he *remembers* your trying to *teach* him to *pronounce* your name. you *will find* he *knows* nothing of it.

And *did* mamma *give* me milk?

Yes, and *nurſed* you night and day.

And *did* you and mamma *teach* me to *ſpeak*?

We *did*. I *took* you upon my knee, and *repeated* to you the words papa and mamma, till you *were* able to *liſp* them: all the words which you *ſpeak* we *taught* you in the ſame manner: you *may remember* that we *taught* you to *read*, and how we *inſtructed* you.

O yes, it *was* a very pretty play.

IX.

Adjectives.

A CHARACTER.

Mary is *obedient* to her parents, *indulgent* to *younger* children, *thankful* for civilities. She is never *tyrannical* over babies, but *obliging* to *all* perſons. She is *dutiful* and *affectionate* to her teachers, *diligent* in her ſtudies, *grateful* to her friends; *mild* and *gentle*, *civil* and *kind*. She is *neat* and *careful*, *amiable* and *agreeable*.—How did ſhe become ſo *charming* a *young* creature?—By following the *good* example of her *worthy* parents, and obſerving the *kind* admonitions of her friends, and being *attentive* to the *excellent* leſſons which ſhe met with in *proper* books.

X.

X

Adverbs

(called Particles.)

Here is a roſe. Come *hither*. *Where* are your ſciſſars? *When* will you learn to keep them? I *often* remind you. *Whence* came this knife? *Now* we can cut ſome, but you ought *always* to loſe your flowers, *when* you are ſo *very* heedleſs. I am *too* indulgent, *indeed* I am. if I were *more* ſtrict, after *once* or *twice*, you would *perhaps* learn to keep your ſciſſars *carefully*, *rather than* loſe your noſegay.

XI

Conjunctions

(called Particles.)

Your papa *and* mamma are going out; *but* you *and* I ſtay at home.

Take pains, *elſe* you cannot learn. Do not hurt, *nor* even frighten any creature

We

We muſt be good, *if* we would be happy.

Unleſs you are an obedient child, you will not be an happy one.

You are older *than* Mary; *yet* ſhe is forwarder *than* you You will be a dunce, *except* you take pains. John is careful, *therefore* he learns quickly. You are ſlow, *becauſe* you are heedleſs. *Although* you could learn, you do not.

XII.

Prepoſitions

(called Particles)

Your papa is going *to* London · he came *from* York yeſterday, he came *in* the coach, becauſe I was *with* him, he will go *into* his new houſe ſoon, there are trees *before* the houſe, and a garden *behind* it.

Take the baſket *off* the table, and ſet my box *upon* it.

Your

Your aunt is *at* Norwich, and will paſs *through* Ipſwich: ſhe is coming *towards* us ſoon; we ſhall be glad to have her *among* us.

Is Pompey *under* the table? Invite him to go *out* of the houſe, and run *in* the garden: he will run *after* you. Do not go *over* the bridge, becauſe he would ſwim *through* the river, and return *into* the houſe wet, and lie *upon* the carpet, and if you go *to* the great lawn, take care *to* keep him *from* the ſheep. he would run *among* the lambs.

PRELUDE TO THE LESSONS IN COLUMNS.

The Manner of uſing the next Set is this:

Take a ſlip of ſtiff paper, or card; place it ſo as to conceal the column of words marked kind.

Read the firſt ſentence, "The ſpider weaves a curious web."

"*What is* The?"—"*An article*"——*You move the ſlip, and the Child ſees he is right.*

There is a third Column for thoſe who are more advanced: for inſtance, the word 'for', *to a very young grammarian it is named particle; to one who is converſant with all the parts of ſpeech, prepoſition, or conjunction, according as it is uſed*——"For *her young*"—*You remind your elder pupil, that* for *here ſhews the relation of the two noun.—the* bird *and her* neſtlings.

Remark

Remark to all, that young *is a noun, because it means* young ones, *or* young birds *it would be an adjective, if the word* birds *were added*

For this set, turn the screen perpendicularly, to conceal the second column

---

LESSONS.

I.

The ſpider weaves a curious web,

Word	Kind.
The	article
ſpider	noun.
weaves	verb
a	article.
curious	adjective.
web	noun

II.

The bird builds a nest for her young—
(meaning nestlings.)

Word	Kind.	Kind:
The	article.	
bird	noun.	
builds	verb.	
a	article.	
nest	noun.	
for	particle	prep.
her	pronoun.	
young (ones)	noun.	

III.

The bee collects both honey and wax
from the flowers.

The	article.
bee	noun.
collects	verb.
both	adjective.
honey	noun.

Word	Kind	Kind
and	particle.	conj
wax	noun.	
from	par.	prep.
the	article.	
flowers	noun	

IV.

The moſt ſavage animals nurſe their offspring with a degree of tenderneſs which ſhames many mothers

The	article	
moſt	particle.	adv.
ſavage	adjective	
animals	noun	
nurſe	verb.	
their	pronoun.	
offspring	noun	
with	particle	prep
a	article	
degree	noun.	
of	particle.	prep

Word	Kind.
tenderness	noun.
which	pronoun.
shames	verb.
many	adjective
mothers	noun

V.

The hen, who from the chilly air,
With pious wing protects her care,
And every fowl that flies at large,
Instructs me in a parent's charge

Word.	Kind.	Kind.
The	article.	def.
hen	noun.	nom.
who	pronoun.	
from	particle	prep.
the	article.	def
chilly	adjective.	
air	noun	
with	particle.	prep.
pious	adjective.	

wing

Word.	Kind.	Kind.
wing	noun.	
protects	verb.	
her	pronoun.	
care *	noun.	
and	particle.	conj
every	adjective.	
fowl	noun.	
that †	pronoun	
flies	verb	
at large ‡	particle.	adv.
instructs	verb.	
me	pronoun.	
in	particle.	prep.
a	article	indef.
parent's	noun.	gen.
charge	noun	

* The objects of her *care*, the chickens

† Meaning *which*.

‡ *Abroad*

VI.

Never confine poor birds forget not that those innocent little creatures were made to enjoy their liberty, and it is very cruel to fill their short life with misery and sorrow

Word	Kind	Kind
Never	particle	adv
confine	verb.	
poor	adjective	
birds	noun.	
forget	verb	
not	particle	adv
that	particle	conj.
those	pronoun	
innocent	adjective.	
little	adjective.	
creatures	noun	
were	verb	
made	particle.	prep.
to	particle	prep.
enjoy	verb.	

their

Word.	Kind	Kind.
their	pronoun	
liberty	noun.	
and	particle.	conj.
that	particle.	conj.
it	pronoun.	
is	verb.	
very	particle.	adv.
cruel	adjective.	
to	particle.	prep.
fill	verb.	
their	pronoun.	
short	adjective.	
life	noun.	
with	particle.	prep.
misery	noun.	
and	particle.	conj.
sorrow.	noun.	

THE following Hymn is designed for Pupils who are sufficiently advanced to distinguish all the different parts of speech, and more particulars respecting them than the younger Students can do Yet for the younger ones it may be used by adverting only to the part of speech marked in the first column; for which reason, all beyond the verb are there denominated particles, *in the next, called by their respective names—for instance,*

for par conj

To be used in portions suited to the Learner —It cannot be too often inculcated, that a little, clearly understood, is best

---

HYMN.

Come, let us praise God, for He is exceedingly great let us bless God; for He is very good.

He made all things, the ſun to rule the day, the moon to ſhine by night.

He made the great whale, and the elephant, and the little worm that crawleth on the ground.

The little birds ſing praiſes to God, when they warble ſweetly in the green ſhade

The brooks and rivers praiſe God, when they murmur melodiouſly among the pebbles

I will praiſe God with my voice, for I may praiſe Him, though I am but a little child

A few years ago, and I was a little infant, and my tongue was dumb within my mouth And I did not know the great name of God, for my reaſon was not come unto me

But now I can ſpeak, and my tongue ſhall praiſe Him, I can think of all His goodneſs, and my heart ſhall love Him

Let

Let Him call me, and I will come unto Him; let Him command, and I will obey Him

When I am older, I will love Him better, and I will never forget God, so long as my life remaineth in me.

Word.	Kind.	Elder
Come	verb.	imp.
let	verb.	verb imp.
us	pron	
praise	verb	
God	noun.	
for	par.	conj
He	pron.	nom.
is	verb.	ind
exceedingly	par.	adv
great	adj.	
let	verb.	verb imp.
us	pron.	
bless	verb.	
God	noun.	
for	par	conj.

He

Word	Kind	Elder
He	pron.	nom. ſing.
is	verb.	ind.
very	par	adv.
good	adj.	
He	pron.	nom ſing maſc. 3.
made	verb.	ind.
all	adj	
things	noun.	
the	art.	def.
ſun	noun.	
to rule	verb.	inf.
day	noun.	
moon	noun	
to ſhine	verb	inf
by	par.	prep
night	noun	
He	pron.	nom. ſing 3 maſ.
made	verb	ind
great	adj	
whale	noun.	
and	par	conj.
little	adj.	

Word	Kind.	Elder.
worm	noun.	
that	pron.	
crawleth	verb.	ind.
upon	par.	prep.
ground	noun.	
little	adj.	
birds	noun.	
ſing	verb.	ind.
praiſes	noun.	
to	par.	prep.
God	noun.	
when	par.	adv.
they	pron.	3 plu.
warble	verb.	ind.
ſweetly	par.	adv.
in	par.	prep.
green	adj	
ſhade	noun.	
brooks	noun.	
and	par.	conj.
rivers	noun.	
praiſe	verb.	ind.

Word.	Kind.	Elder
God	noun.	
when	par	adv.
they	pron.	nom.
murmur	verb.	ind
melodiously	par.	adv.
amongst	par.	prep.
smooth	adj.	
pebbles	noun.	
I	pron.	sing nom. 1.
will	verb.	} ind.
praise	verb	
God	noun.	
with	par.	prep.
my	pron.	
voice	noun.	
for	par	conj
I	pron.	nom. sing 1.
may	verb	} pot.
praise	verb.	
Him	pron.	acc masc 3 sing.
though	par.	conj.
I	pron	nom. sing 1.

Word	Kind	Elder
am	verb.	ind
but	par	conj
little	adj	
child	noun.	
few	adj.	
years	noun.	
ago	par.	adv.
and	par.	conj.
I	pron.	nom. ſing. 1.
was	verb.	ind.
a little infant and	as before	
my	pron.	
tongue	noun.	
was	verb.	ind.
dumb	adj.	
within	par.	prep.
my	pron.	poſſeſſive
mouth	noun.	
and I	as before.	
did	verb.	
not	par.	adv } indicative.
know	verb.	

the

Word	Kind.	Elder
the great	as before	
name	noun.	
of	par.	prep
God	noun.	
for (becauſe)	par.	conj.
my	pron	
reaſon	noun.	
was	verb.	ind.
not	par	adv
come	verb.	participle
unto	par	prep.
me	pron.	acc ſing 1.
but	par.	conj.
now	par	adv.
I	pron	ſing nom. 1
can	verb	} potential
ſpeak	verb.	
my	pron	poſſ 1 ſing.
tongue	noun.	
ſhall	verb.	} indic.
praiſe	verb.	
Him	pron.	3 acc. ſing. m.

Word.	Kind.	Elder.
I	pron.	1 nom. ſing.
can	verb.	potential.
think	verb.	
of	par.	prep.
all	adj.	
His	pron.	poſſ. 3 ſing. m.
kindneſs	noun.	
and my	as before.	
heart	noun.	
ſhall love	verb.	indic.
Him	pron.	ſing. acc. maſ. 3.
let	verb.	verb imper.
Him	pron.	
call	verb.	
me	pron.	ſing acc. 1.
I	pron.	ſing nom. 1.
will come	verb	indic.
unto	par.	prep.
let	verb.	imper. 3d ſing.
Him	pron.	
command	verb.	
and I will obey Him	as before.	

When

Word.	Kind.	Elder
When	par.	adv.
I	pron.	ſing. nom. 1.
am	verb.	
older	adj.	compar.
I will praiſe	verb.	indic.
Him	pron.	ſing. acc. maſ 3.
better	adverb—ſhewing the manner of the verb—compar.	
and I will	as before.	
never	par	adv.
forget	verb.	
God	noun.	
ſo long	par.	adv.
as	par.	conj.
my	pron.	poſſ. ſing 1.
life	noun.	
remaineth	verb.	
in	par.	prep.
me	pron.	ſing. acc 1.

QUERIES,

QUERIES,

FOR EXAMINATION OF PUPILS IN GRAMMAR.

WHAT part of ſpeech?
Why is it ſo?
To what accidents is it ſubject?

1. *Article.*

Definite, or indefinite?

(Mother's Gram. 11)

2. *Noun.*

Kind?—proper, or common?
Number?—ſingular, or plural?
Caſe?—nominative, or genitive?
Gender?—maſculine, feminine, or neuter?

3. *Ad-*

3. *Adjective.*

Degree?—positive, comparative, or superlative?

4. *Pronoun.*

Case?—nominative, accusative, or a possessive pronoun?

Gender?—masculine, feminine, or neuter?

Person?—First, second, or third?

5. *Verb.*

Number?—singular, or plural?

Person?—first, second, or third?

Mode?—indicative, imperative, subjunctive, or infinitive?

Tense?—past, present, or future?

Past.—Preterimperfect, preterperfect, or preterpluperfect?

Future.—Future imperfect? or future perfect.

6. *Par-*

6. *Participle.*

(Mother's Gram. 48.

Active, or paſſive?—What kind?

7. *Adverb.*

What kind?—poſitive, comparative, or ſuperlative?

The reſt are undeclined.

A

SERIES OF BOOKS FOR TEACHING.

SOLD BY

E. NEWBERY, St. Paul's Church-Yard

1 THE Infant's Friend—Part I.—A Spelling Book, &c.—Price 8d.

2 The Infant's Friend—Part II.—Reading Lessons for young Children, &c —Price 1s.

3. The Child's Grammar —Price 6d.

4. Parsing Lessons for young Children: resolved into their Elements, for the Assistance of Parents and Teachers —Price 9d.

5 The Mother's Grammar —Price 6d.

6 Parsing Lessons for elder Pupils Resolved into their Elements, with Rules for Parsing, &c &c.

SCHEMES

SCHEMES FOR TEACHING,

Under the Idea of

AMUSEMENT.

The Infant's Delight, a Specimen of Plates in a ſuperior Stile for Children; with a Book containing a Liſt of their Names; forming a Set of Leſſons in reading as Rewards; and an Addreſs to Mothers. in an engraved caſe —Price 1s 6d.

The Figure Scheme; or, Figures rendered Pleaſant to Children: in a bag, 3s —in a box, with cuts as douceurs, 6s.

At Mrs NEWBERY's alſo may be had,

A Short Hiſtory of Inſects; containing Rudiments; deſigned as an Introduction to the Study of that Branch of Natural Hiſtory, and as a Pocket Companion to thoſe who viſit Muſeums: with a Frontiſpiece, explanatory of Diſtinctions, and a Plate to each Order, containing one example of each Genus in that Order—Uncoloured and ſewed, 3s. 6d.

The Village Matron, or Anecdotes, &c.—1s.

The Sunday Miſcellany, in Proſe and Verſe, for Young Perſons.—1s.

Lightning Source UK Ltd.
Milton Keynes UK
UKOW05f1859191217
314784UK00008B/973/P

9 781140 699958